WHY MONEY WAS INVENTED

Neale S. Godfrey

The One-and-Only Common Sense ^cents Series ™

Illustrated by
Randy Verougstraete

Silver Press
Parsippany, New Jersey

In loving memory of Sophie. You're always in my thoughts and in my heart.
Love, Neale

The art in this book is dedicated to my friends Sean and Roman.
Randy Verougstraete

 Published simultaneously by Silver Press and Modern Curriculum Press,
Divisions of Simon & Schuster.
299 Jefferson Road, Parsippany, NJ 07054

Design/Cover by Michelle Farinella

All photos © Silver Burdett Ginn
Printed in Mexico
1 2 3 4 5 6 7 8 9 10   00 99 98 97 96 95

Library of Congress Cataloging-in-Publication Data
Godfrey, Neale S.
Why Money was Invented/by Neale S. Godfrey;
Illustrated by Randy Verougstraete.
p. cm.—(One and only common cents series)
Summary: The GreenStreet$ Kids learn about the invention of money,
beginning with the concept of bartering, or trading to obtain goods,
through the use of precious metals and eventually to coins and paper money.
I. Money—History—Juvenile literature. [I. Money—History.]
I. Verougstraete, Randy, ill. II. Title III. Series.
HG221.5.G634 1995   94-39823   332.4'9—dc20   CIP   AC
ISBN 0-382-24914-3 (LSB)
ISBN 0-382-24913-5 (JHC)
ISBN 0-8136-0585-7 (SC)

For each book that is sold,
Simon & Schuster Education Group
and the author of this book,
Neale S. Godfrey,
along with Children's Financial Network,
will jointly contribute 25¢ to
the U.S. Committee for UNICEF
to help children around the world.

United States Committee for

 **unicef**

United Nations Children's Fund
333 East 38th St., New York, NY 10016

It was summer in the town of Green$treet$.
Everyone was having a great time in the park.
The Green$treet$ Kids were having a race.

3

Penny Bright,

Dollar Bill, better known as Buck,

Hedge, Small Change,

Short Cut, and

Ona Budget

were all in the race.

Ona Budget was the first one to cross the finish line.

FINISH LINE

After the race, everyone rested on the grass.

5

Then Short Cut tried to trade his sandwich for Buck's popcorn.

Just then, everyone heard the bell of an ice-cream truck.

"That's what I really want—ice cream," said Short Cut.

"Me too," added Ona.

"Me three!" exclaimed Small Change.

Everyone ran toward the ice-cream truck.

"Mr. Bear, will you trade these marbles for ice-cream cones?" Short Cut asked eagerly.

Bear shook his head. "I won't trade ice cream for marbles," he said.

"Here," said Small Change, "I have a lot of money."

"Nice try," said Penny, "but that won't even buy us the sprinkles."

"I don't understand why Mr. Bear wouldn't take my marbles," questioned Short Cut.

"You see, Short Cut, trading doesn't always work," explained Hedge.

"That's why money was invented," added Penny.

"Money was invented?" Short Cut asked.

"Even small change?" questioned Small Change.

"Yes, money was invented a long, long time ago," replied Penny.

·BILLBOARD·
Did you ever have a new idea?
New ideas are sometimes
called **inventions**.
Maybe you've invented something!

"Let me tell you about it.
First, close your eyes and imagine that we all lived long, long ago . . . ."

11

Long ago, people did not have money.
They traded things they had for
things they needed or wanted.

· BILLBOARD ·

Did you ever trade stickers
with your friends?
If so, you were bartering!
Bartering is another name for trading.

13

But trading wasn't always easy.
In hot weather, some things spoiled.
Imagine milk sitting in the hot sun.

Heavy things were hard to carry.
Imagine how hard it would be to carry a sack of stones.

Sometimes, people had to travel a long way to trade things.
Can you imagine traveling very far with wriggling pigs?

Later on, people found other ways to trade.
They could trade their work for something
they needed or wanted.

Let's say a person needed new shoes.
He could pay for the shoes by doing
some work for the shoemaker.

Maybe someone wanted bread.
She could pay for the bread by doing some work for the baker.

If a person needed a coat, he could work for the tailor.
Then he would be working to pay for the coat.

When people were trading, they would bargain with each other. If they couldn't agree, then there wouldn't be a trade!

Some trades worked.
Some trades didn't.

But there were problems with trading.
People didn't always have what someone else wanted.
Some people started to use things like shells, feathers,
or beads as a way to buy things.

But sometimes even those things didn't work.
Shells cracked.
Feathers flew.
Beads rolled away.

Through the years, different people had different ideas.

They decided to use lumps of metal, such as gold and silver. Pieces of metal were easy to carry and weren't changed by hot or cold weather.
But the metals did have to be weighed and measured every time they were used.

-BILLBOARD-

All of these metals were used for money!

Gold • Silver • Bronze • Copper
Iron • Lead • Tin

23

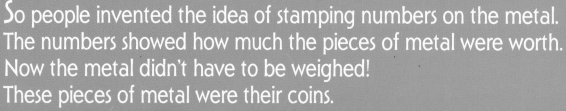

So people invented the idea of stamping numbers on the metal.
The numbers showed how much the pieces of metal were worth.
Now the metal didn't have to be weighed!
These pieces of metal were their coins.

People decided to make money out of paper, too.
They printed the value on the paper.
Everyone agreed to use the paper as money.

This is the perfect type of money. It fits right into my wallet!

·BILLBOARD·
The first paper money was made in China.
China didn't have enough metal to make coins for its millions of people.
So paper money was invented.

25

People all over the world invented their own money.
Each country had its own special pictures on the money.
The pictures told about a country's people and places.

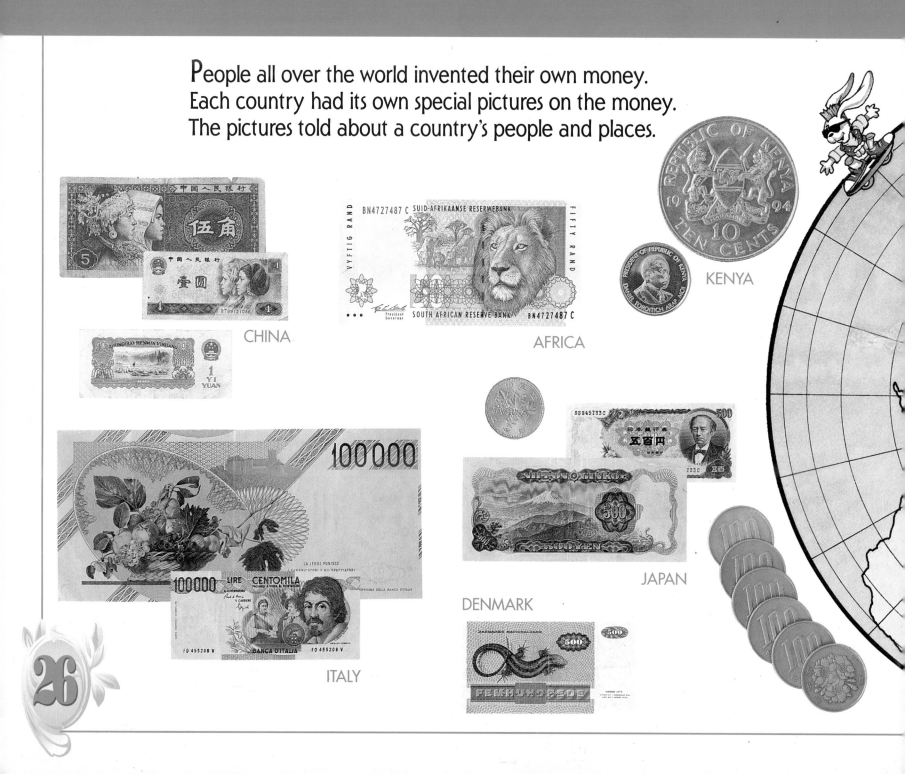

KENYA

CHINA

AFRICA

JAPAN

DENMARK

ITALY

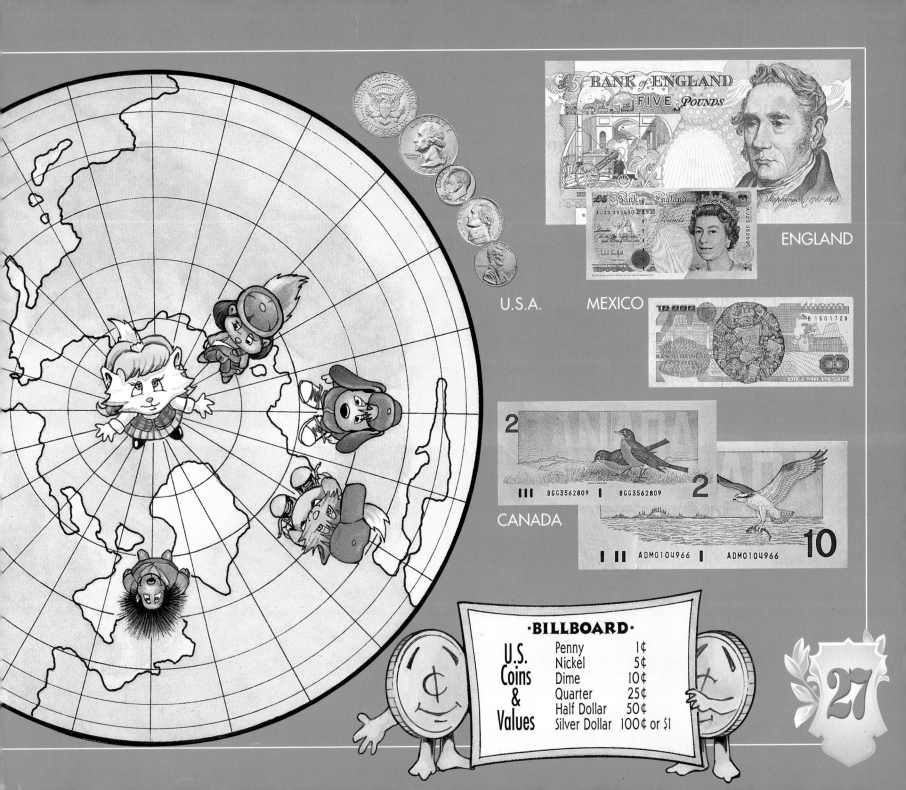

U.S.A.

MEXICO

ENGLAND

CANADA

·BILLBOARD·

U.S. Coins & Values		
Penny	1¢
Nickel	5¢
Dime	10¢
Quarter	25¢
Half Dollar	50¢
Silver Dollar	100¢ or $1

27

"Wow! I never knew money was invented. I thought it was just there," said Buck.

"It's a good thing it was invented," said Small Change. "Otherwise, what would I put in my change maker?"

"And now I understand why my trading won't always work," agreed Short Cut. "But I still want ice cream."

"We still don't have the money to buy it," said Buck.

"I have an idea," said Penny.
"Let's try to earn the money."

·BILLBOARD·
Do you have a piggy bank?
The first piggy banks were made
from a clay called **pygg**.
Later the banks were made to look like pigs
and were called **piggy banks**.

29

So the Green$treet$ Kids got busy.

And they worked the whole afternoon.

"We're back, Mr. Bear," said Buck.
"This time we have money for ice cream."

Mr. Bear sold ice cream to everyone.

"This ice cream is delicious!" the kids cheered.

"It was worth working for!"

"Right," said Penny, "and all we used was common sense!"